Acting Edition

Off Off Broadway Festival Plays, 48th Series

18
by Darius M. Buckley

Drawbridge
by Mallory Jane Weiss

Dugout Daisies
by Julissa Mishay Norment

Freestyle Hand Entry
by Elise Wien

Nub City, USA!
by Nicholas Hulstine

The Velociraptor's Very Good Day
by Sarah Kaufman & Shane Dittmar

‖SAMUEL FRENCH‖

18 © 2024 by Darius M. Buckley
Drawbridge © 2024 by Mallory Jane Weiss
Dugout Daisies © 2024 by Julissa Mishay Norment
Freestyle Hand Entry © 2024 by Elise Wien
Nub City, USA! © 2024 by Nicholas Hulstine
The Velociraptor's Very Good Day © 2024
by Sarah Kaufman & Shane Dittmar
All Rights Reserved

OFF OFF BROADWAY FESTIVAL PLAYS, 48TH SERIES is fully protected under the copyright laws of the United States of America, the British Commonwealth, including Canada, and all member countries of the Berne Convention for the Protection of Literary and Artistic Works, the Universal Copyright Convention, and/or the World Trade Organization conforming to the Agreement on Trade Related Aspects of Intellectual Property Rights. All rights, including professional and amateur stage productions, recitation, lecturing, public reading, motion picture, radio broadcasting, television, online/digital production, and the rights of translation into foreign languages are strictly reserved.

ISBN 978-0-573-71122-0

www.concordtheatricals.com
www.concordtheatricals.co.uk

FOR PRODUCTION INQUIRIES
UNITED STATES AND CANADA
info@concordtheatricals.com
1-866-979-0447

UNITED KINGDOM AND EUROPE
licensing@concordtheatricals.co.uk
020-7054-7298

Each title is subject to availability from Concord Theatricals Corp., depending upon country of performance. Please be aware that *OFF OFF BROADWAY FESTIVAL PLAYS, 48TH SERIES* may not be licensed by Concord Theatricals Corp. in your territory. Professional and amateur producers should contact the nearest Concord Theatricals Corp. office or licensing partner to verify availability.

CAUTION: Professional and amateur producers are hereby warned that *OFF OFF BROADWAY FESTIVAL PLAYS, 48TH SERIES* is subject to a licensing fee. The purchase, renting, lending or use of this book does not constitute a license to perform this title(s), which license must be obtained from Concord Theatricals Corp. prior to any performance. Performance of this title(s) without a license is a violation of federal law and may subject the producer and/or presenter of such performances to civil penalties. Both amateurs and professionals considering a production are strongly advised to apply to the appropriate agent before starting rehearsals, advertising, or booking a theatre. A licensing fee must be paid whether the title(s) is presented for charity or gain and whether or not admission is charged. Professional/Stock licensing fees are quoted upon application to Concord Theatricals Corp.

This work is published by Samuel French, an imprint of Concord Theatricals Corp.

No one shall make any changes in this title(s) for the purpose of production. No part of this book may be reproduced, stored in a retrieval system, scanned, uploaded, or transmitted in any form, by any means, now known or yet to be invented, including mechanical, electronic, digital, photocopying, recording, videotaping, or otherwise, without the prior written permission of the publisher. No one shall share this title(s), or any part of this title(s), through any social media or file hosting websites.

For all inquiries regarding motion picture, television, online/digital and other media rights, please contact Concord Theatricals Corp.

MUSIC AND THIRD-PARTY MATERIALS USE NOTE

Licensees are solely responsible for obtaining formal written permission from copyright owners to use copyrighted music and/or other copyrighted third-party materials (e.g. artworks, logos) in the performance of this play and are strongly cautioned to do so. If no such permission is obtained by the licensee, then the licensee must use only original music and materials that the licensee owns and controls. Licensees are solely responsible and liable for clearances of all third-party copyrighted materials, including without limitation music, and shall indemnify the copyright owners of the play(s) and their licensing agent, Concord Theatricals Corp., against any costs, expenses, losses and liabilities arising from the use of such copyrighted third-party materials by licensees. For music, please contact the appropriate music licensing authority in your territory for the rights to any incidental music.

IMPORTANT BILLING AND CREDIT REQUIREMENTS

If you have obtained performance rights to this title, please refer to your licensing agreement for important billing and credit requirements.

Concord Theatricals presents The Samuel French Off Off Broadway Short Play Festival (OOB) has been the nation's leading short play festival for forty-eight years. The OOB Festival has served as a doorway to future success for aspiring writers. Over two hundred plays have been published, and many participants have become established, award-winning playwrights.

For more information on the Off Off Broadway Short Play Festival, including history, interviews, and more, please visit www.oobfestival.com.

HONORARY GUEST PLAYWRIGHT
James Ijames

2023 FESTIVAL JUDGES
Jason Aguirre
Christina Anderson
Hilary Bettis
Eleanor Burgess
Steph Del Rosso
Jason Eagan
Skylar Fox
Gracie Gardner
Margaret Ledford
Jill Rafson
Jonathan Silverstein
Emmanuel Wilson

Festival Sponsor: Concord Theatricals

Festival Artistic Director: Casey McLain

Literary Director/Opening Night Party Moderator: Garrett Anderson

Festival Host/Client Manager: Abbie Van Nostrand

House Manager: Tyler Mullen

Box Office Manager: Rosemary Bucher

Marketing Team: Meredith Foster, Jeremiah Hernandez, Courtney Kochuba, and Imogen Lloyd Webber

Festival Production Coordinators: Cambria Martin, Clare Rankine, and Alexandra Varitek

Festival Support Staff: Ella Andrew, Victoria Bond, Meredith Foster, Shaina Gilks, Jeremiah Hernandez, Ben Keiper, Rachel Levens, David McMaines, Gabriela Morales, Nate Netzley, Kristen Rea, Rachel Smith, and Faith Williams

2023 Submissions Readers: Ella Andrew, Caroline Barnard, Caroline Bohnenberger, Jim Colleran, Charlie Coulthard, Sequoyah Douglas, Meredith Foster, Marquis Hardin, Rachel Levens, Amy Rose Marsh, Debbie McLean, David McMaines, Elizabeth Minski, Gabriela Morales, Tyler Mullen, Alexander Perez, Kristen Rea, Rachel Smith, Abbie Van Nostrand, Sarah Weber, and Faith Williams

Special Thanks: Sean Flahaven, Bill Gaden, Concord Theatricals, and City Theatre Miami

About Concord Theatricals

Concord Theatricals is the world's most significant theatrical company, comprising the catalogs of R&H Theatricals, Samuel French, Tams-Witmark, and The Andrew Lloyd Webber Collection, plus dozens of new signings each year.

Our unparalleled roster includes the work of Irving Berlin, Agatha Christie, George & Ira Gershwin, Marvin Hamlisch, Lorraine Hansberry, Jeremy O. Harris, Kander & Ebb, Tom Kitt, Ken Ludwig, Marlow & Moss, Lin-Manuel Miranda, Anaïs Mitchell, Dominique Morisseau, Cole Porter, Theresa Rebeck, Rodgers & Hammerstein, Thornton Wilder, and August Wilson. We are the only firm providing truly comprehensive services to the creators and producers of plays and musicals, including theatrical licensing, music publishing, script publishing, cast recording, and first-class production.

TABLE OF CONTENTS

Foreword	ix
18 by Darius M. Buckley	1
Drawbridge by Mallory Jane Weiss	19
Dugout Daisies by Julissa Mishay Norment	31
Freestyle Hand Entry by Elise Wien	47
Nub City, USA! by Nicholas Hulstine	57
The Velociraptor's Very Good Day by Sarah Kaufman & Shane Dittmar	69

FOREWORD

Concord Theatricals is honored to have the six daring and inspirational playwrights included in this collection as the winners of our 48th Annual Off Off Broadway Short Play Festival. This year our festival received eight hundred and fifty submissions from around the world. We thank all of these gifted playwrights for sharing their talent with us and welcome each writer into our elite group of Off Off Broadway Festival winners.

This year's festival was an extraordinary showcase of creativity and artistry, owing its greatness to the sheer talent and ingenuity of the playwrights involved.

From our initial pool of Top-Thirty playwrights, we ultimately select six plays for publication and representation by Concord Theatricals. Of course, we can't make our selections alone, so we enlist some brilliant minds within the theatre industry to help us in this process. We invited an esteemed group of twelve judges consisting of a mix of Concord Theatricals playwrights and members of the theatre industry. We thank them for their support, insight, and commitment to the art of playwriting.

We are constantly striving to develop groundbreaking methods that will better connect playwright and producer. With a team committed to continuing our tradition of publishing and licensing the best new theatrical works, we are boldly embracing our role in this industry as bridge between playwright and theatre.

On behalf of the entire Concord Theatricals team in our New York, London, and Berlin offices, and the over ten thousand playwrights, composers, and lyricists that we publish and represent, we present you with the six winning plays of the 48th Annual Samuel French Off Off Broadway Short Play Festival.

This festival is about playwrights. Sharing the human story. We invite you to enjoy these extraordinary plays.

Casey McLain and Garrett Anderson
Artistic Director and Literary Director
The Samuel French Off Off Broadway Short Play Festival

18

A Short Play in Verse

by Darius M. Buckley

18 was first produced by the 48th Annual Samuel French Off Off Broadway Play Festival at the Vineyard Theater in New York City in August 2023. The performance was directed by Catalina Beltrán and produced by David O'Brien. The cast was as follows:

JAY.. DJ Davis
TREYVON.. Austin Sasser

CHARACTERS

JAY – Seventeen years old (can be played by a teenager or young adult), African American, imaginative, a poet.

TREYVON – Seventeen years old (can be played by a teenager or young adult), African American, passionate, a high school basketball player.

SETTING

New York café and New York Youth Corrections Facility.

TIME

Present.

Scene One

(SETTING: A room that feels like a café. There are tables and chairs everywhere, except for the open space in the center that serves as a stage with two mic stands.)

*(AT RISE: The audience takes their seats. There's coffee or tea on the tables, the room is bustling when **JAY** and **TREYVON** enter. They both take a breath in unison.)*

JAY & TREYVON. Breathe.

JAY. That's what they told Momma when she was performing her miracle on August 16, 2005.

TREYVON. Push...

JAY. Though the pain was so intense that the angels had to hold her hands.

TREYVON. Push...

JAY. Promising a new hope on the other side of the doctor's negligence.

TREYVON. Push...

JAY. Medicine was all she asked for.

TREYVON. Push...

JAY. Cus the pain was too intense, even for a warrior like her.

TREYVON. Push...

JAY. "Please sir, just something to ease the pain."

TREYVON. "People like you are all the same...push..."

JAY. "Something to take away the stinging in my chest."

TREYVON. "You'll be treated like all the rest, bare the pain and push..."

JAY. "My heart shouldn't beat like this, my skin is on fire."

TREYVON. "When you grow tired it'll all fade away, just do as I say..."

JAY. She gripped the sheets and let out one last war cry before the head emerged...

TREYVON. Hold on...

JAY. And she heard the wail of a new life submerged under the sheets.

TREYVON. What a sight to see...

JAY. It was me, warm and mad as hell that I'd been taken from my safe haven. The womb was the only place where the law didn't affect me.

TREYVON. They reached in and pulled out the yolk of afterbirth, the slime of life, and when the time was right...

JAY. They placed me in her arms, and I looked up at a small brown skinned woman with years of pain and love on her face.

Not a trace of regret, only wonder for the miracle she had just performed. A divine act from Saint Lucinda. The woman who gave me life.

TREYVON. May he have it more abundantly.

JAY. Life.

TREYVON. With years of sorrow shrouded by the grace of God.

JAY. Life.

TREYVON. May he find it in the most surprising places.

JAY. Life.

TREYVON. Let him find peace in the staff and the rod… may they comfort him.

>*(Lights shift as **TREYVON** takes the stage for himself, **JAY** sits down to make room for his brother. The space grows a little tighter.)*

Scene Two

*(**TREYVON** smiles and closes his eyes. We hear the sound of Central Park as a distant echo.)*

TREYVON. The last thing I remember about my girl was her smell. She used to wear Bath & Body Works' Japanese Cherry Blossom, and I swear, when I leaned against her, I could hear the trees rustling in Central Park.

Pink petals falling on her shoulders like snow.

She was like a tree, cus her roots kept me grounded.

Her arms, like branches wrapped around me, and I never wanted her to let go.

Little did she know the grip she had on me.

I was hooked, and she wasn't even trying, it was just her

Nature.

Natural beauty wrapped around a perfect soul.

She was more beautiful than you'll ever know.

And I think of her beauty every time I close my eyes, and smell those sweet blossoms.

I see them drifting through the sky, then down on her shoulder,

I hold her,

I kiss her.

She squeezes my shoulders and looks up at me with those warm brown eyes and I melt, cus there ain't a girl in this city that can come close to my Sydney.

I just hope she remembers me...

*(**JAY** gets up and moves around the room. **TREYVON** gives him his focus.)*

Scene Three

(We hear the distant sounds of New York: trains, traffic, people.)

JAY. I'm a writer.

I write magic on white surfaces that turn into vibrant worlds of texture and color.

Rhyme and reason.

Reflections of the lives we live and love we give,

I was a poet.

I could write universes with my words.

A place to escape when the streets became too much.

When the bullies became too much.

When the loss of Dad became...

I could write healing in syllables, medicine in the stanzas of poems that could stand with the greats.

They called me young Langston Hughes.

A magician with a pen and a dream,

that couldn't lose steam,

he just keeps going,

he just keeps writing until he's out.

Until Momma is out.

Until all of this is a memory.

Until we're living in condos on the Upper West Side,

sipping tea on rooftop terraces,

where rich white folks stare at us,

cus how did these niggas make it to a place like this?

I wrote us out.

Scene Four

> (**TREYVON** *and* **JAY** *sit across the room from each other.*)

JAY. I remember when I used to have dreams.

In the summertime they came with ease.

The open window next to my bed would welcome in that cool night breeze.

With the smell of late night soul food from the restaurant below.

The rumble of the C underneath my feet.

Like a train taking my bed to some other world where grass was greener and trees were tall like skyscrapers.

TREYVON. Oh yeah?

JAY. I'm telling you Trey, I used to dream.

I saw things you only see on the big screen.

I saw mountains taller than Everest.

Oceans deeper than the Atlantic.

Moons and stars as far as the eyes could reach,

And when I reached out I could pull down the sun.

TREYVON. The whole sun? In one reach?

JAY. Nigga, I could fly up ten thousand feet.

I had wings Trey.

Like some shit you see in storybooks or on HBO.

Bro, I was magical and shit.

TREYVON. Magical? Nigga please.

JAY. I had wings, and God knows if I could stretch 'em out now, we'd be outta this place...

TREYVON. Yeah?

JAY. I'd lift you up in my arms and...

> We'd be flying over the gated basketball court,
>
> With Corey and Mike's bitch asses looking up from below,
>
> Like how did that nigga get wings?!

TREYVON. Probably be the craziest shit they've ever seen!

JAY. Gliding over Sugar Hill and leaping off of the Empire State.

TREYVON. Like Spiderman nigga?

JAY. Naw Trey, like me.

> That nigga ain't got nothing on me.
>
> He ain't got nothing on the dreams I used to dream.

TREYVON. Shit must've been sweet...

JAY. Shit was crazy Trey.

> I didn't wanna wake up.
>
> I would go to bed early just to drift off.
>
> Just to see what was on the other side of those tall trees.
>
> Just past the glass mountains of lower Manhattan.
>
> I'd see trees, trees as tall as outer space.
>
> Tall with twisted long brown branches.
>
> Like hands that reached out across the world.

TREYVON. The whole thing?

JAY. The whole thing...

> Bro, I told you it was a dream.
>
> The type of shit you can't define.

TREYVON. Well I should tell you about mine...

JAY. Man you used to dream too?!

TREYVON. Nigga, they thought I was dead when I was sleep.

Dreams had my ass knocked out deep.

At night I saw crazy things.

JAY. Crazier than a tree with arms?

> *(We hear the sound of a storm. Immersive, one that grows in intensity throughout the monologue.)*

TREYVON. I was standing in the ocean.

And I saw a storm coming in the distance.

Big clouds and big waves.

Like a hurricane...

Barreling toward me at the speed of light.

JAY. This sounds like a nightmare...

TREYVON. The kind that makes you say a prayer after.

I was tense.

My arms were sweaty and my palms cold.

My body didn't know what temperature to be.

I was frozen at sea.

Feeling the water rush between my legs.

I could see my dad on the other side yelling my name.

"Treyvon! Treyvon!"

It was too late for me to be saved.

I felt the wind and...crash!

The wave hit me and I swung under the tide.

I woke up in sweats that night.

JAY. What happened next?

TREYVON. I ended up here...

JAY. You ended up here?

TREYVON. It was the night before everything...

Scene Five

(The space grows tighter.)

JAY. July 4, 2021 was the night that everything changed. It was the night that I was arrested for a crime I didn't commit.

TREYVON. It was the night I was arrested for a misunderstanding.

JAY. We were just foolin' around.

TREYVON. We were just foolin' around.

JAY. I wasn't even the guy that did it.

TREYVON. I didn't realize what had happened until it was too late.

JAY. Devon was a bully.

TREYVON. Trevor was a menace. I swear that nigga could make a pacifist beat his ass.

JAY. He spent the whole night talking shit. Talking mad shit and acted surprised when Carter checked him.

TREYVON. He was feeling real froggy until my boy got a little jump in him.

JAY. Then he wanted to back down like a bitch.

TREYVON. His bark was just as whiney as his bite, nothing real behind it, he was a fuckin' punk.

JAY. I kept myself in the back for most of the fight.

TREYVON. I didn't want any smoke, I had done everything I could to gain Dad's trust again.

JAY. I had done everything I could to make Momma proud.

TREYVON. Dad kept saying, "We can't keep bailing you out Trey."

JAY. "You have too much to lose Jay, choose your friends wisely."

TREYVON. "College recruits have their eyes on you, you could change things for this family."

JAY. "A full ride to NYU Jay, you're opening doors for the boys in this family that come behind you."

TREYVON. "Don't fuck this up Trey."

JAY. "Don't lose your focus Jay."

TREYVON. "Leave that street shit for the rats, boy."

JAY. "You're built different than them, don't forget that, son."

TREYVON. "You could get out."

JAY. "You could get out."

TREYVON. I didn't get out.

JAY. I didn't get out.

TREYVON. One blow to the head...

JAY. One moment too long in the parking lot...

TREYVON. He was talking shit about my Momma, you gotta understand.

JAY. I didn't even do anything... I was just the last one that didn't get away.

TREYVON. I didn't think I hit him that hard.

JAY. It wasn't my fault.

TREYVON. He pulled out a gun. He threatened my life. It's like everything went in slow motion.

JAY. I was almost home.

TREYVON. Large white hands snatched me back into reality.

JAY. My face was slammed on the warm concrete. Blood rushing like an ocean.

TREYVON. A knee on my neck. I swear I couldn't breathe.

JAY. Momma!

TREYVON. I cried out but I felt like nobody could hear me.

JAY. Jesus!

TREYVON. Momma always said, "Cry out to Jesus when I'm not there. He'll hear you first..."

JAY. Jesus!

TREYVON. Momma was gone, so *He* was all I had.

JAY. Jesus...

TREYVON. I fell unconscious...and that's all I can remember.

JAY. That's all I can remember.

TREYVON. The night everything changed.

JAY. The night my life was taken away.

Scene Six

(The space in the room grows tighter.)

TREYVON. Young black male, 5'11, one scar under his left eye, muscular build, resistant, significant history of prior offenses.

JAY. Young black male, 5'9, slim build, quiet but suspicious, no history of prior offenses.

TREYVON. On the night of July 4, 2021 Treyvon Carter was found at the scene of the crime, standing over the victim, breathing heavy, eyes wide as if he was on drugs. The suspect resisted arrest and was aggressively verbal until he was forced to the ground by Officer Travis and eventually loosened his grip.

JAY. Jayson Tyler claims he was not responsible for the attack on the victim but had dodgy eye movement and spoke quickly. When Officer Kisner attempted to handcuff the suspect, he began crying and what seems like praying. He was pinned to the ground and began screaming "Jesus" for five minutes until he eventually stopped and relaxed his muscles.

TREYVON. The suspect's parent neglected to come to the police station after the arrest.

JAY. The suspect's mother was quite angry and threatened legal action when called by Officer Kisner.

TREYVON. The suspect was not very cooperative during questioning.

JAY. The suspect was tearful during questioning.

TREYVON. The suspect has been moved from the Bronx Youth Corrections Facility.

JAY. The suspect is being prepared for their transition to the Brooklyn Corrections Center, an adult facility.

TREYVON. This documentation will be forwarded to the corrections team at the new facility.

JAY. Please feel free to contact us for any suggestions on community integration for both young men.

TREYVON. The bus will be taking six of the young men from our facility on Tuesday.

JAY. Jayson Tyler's mother will be present at the transition.

TREYVON. Appeals have been filed.

JAY. Appeals will be denied.

TREYVON. Be firm.

JAY. Be gentle.

TREYVON. Stand your ground.

JAY. Get on their level.

TREYVON. Signed...

JAY. Officer Fischer.

TREYVON. Inmate photos attached.

JAY. Download JPG file.

TREYVON. Inmate 234.

JAY. Inmate 756.

(Blackout.)

End of Play

Drawbridge

by Mallory Jane Weiss

DRAWBRIDGE was first produced by the 48th Annual Samuel French Off Off Broadway Play Festival at the Vineyard Theater in New York City in August 2023. The performance was directed by Lily Kanter Riopelle. The cast was as follows:

DOOR . . . . Collin McConnell
TUESDAY . . . . Frankie Placidi

CHARACTERS

The Drawbridge Lowerers

DOOR – driven by practical ambition
TUESDAY – overflowing with curious mischief

SETTING

A drawbridge to the castle
Somewhere very far from the next town over,
and very far from everywhere.

TIME

An anachronistic late fifteenth century

"The limits of my language mean the limits of my world."
– Ludwig Wittgenstein

The Lexicographer Is on Their Way

*(**DOOR** and **TUESDAY** in the gatehouse at the drawbridge of the castle.)*

*(**TUESDAY** pulls on the rope, messing with its frayed end.)*

DOOR. Don't fidget with that. You'll break it.

And if you break it, we won't be able to lower the bridge.

And if we can't lower the bridge, the Lexicographer will have to knock.

And after they knock, we'll have to yell down, "Sorry, we broke the thing!"

And the Lexicographer will shake their head and think, "Such foolish fools hardly deserve the fruits of my cart," and they will turn right around and leave our village without bestowing upon us so much as a tiny little noun.

And then, we'll have to go to the king and explain what happened...that there was a dangling thing, and we couldn't help but play with it because, apparently, we're housecats. Yes, I said "we," because I would never leave you to face the king alone. Remember that.

And then we'll tell our whole tale, and the king will sit back in his throne, and take a sip of his wine and a nibble of his croissant (which will have gone limp in this humidity and will certainly sour his mood further),

and then he will

behead us.

TUESDAY. You're acting like there's a bear and you're holding a ham sandwich.

(**DOOR** *takes the rope out of* **TUESDAY**'s *hands.*)

DOOR. Tie your shoe.

(**TUESDAY** *ties their undone shoelace.* **DOOR** *uses binoculars to look out.*)

That thing on the end of your lace?

That's called an "aglet." Did you know that?

The Lexicographer brought us that one last harvest season, but I think it's gone underutilized. I think we could use another one like that this time. A word for the tip of the tree branch, perhaps.

TUESDAY. Twig?

DOOR. A twig is once it's fallen.

TUESDAY. I heard a rumor, actually.

About what dear ole Lexi's going to bring us this time.

...

Don't you want to know the rumor?

DOOR. Is the source reputable?

TUESDAY. I heard it at the mead hall.

DOOR. So, no.

TUESDAY. It's *feelings*.

DOOR. What?

TUESDAY. They're bringing us feelings.

DOOR. We already have feelings.

TUESDAY. No, the words for them.

DOOR. We have those.

TUESDAY. Name four.

DOOR. Happy, sad

Angry.

...

TUESDAY. See?

DOOR. Hold on hold on

The one you just said before when I was saying "don't play with the thing"?

Like there's a bear, and I'm holding a ham sandwich. It's like angry and sad. Put together. Like, being angry that you're sad. Or sad that you're angry. There isn't a word for that though.

TUESDAY. Apparently, there is. I heard that they're bringing us a whole cart's worth. And some of them are really sharp and big. And there's one other thing, but you aren't going to like it.

DOOR. Then don't tell me.

TUESDAY. They're magic!

When you use them, something happens, like

there's a kind of alchemy. Like, it's like putting water in a pot over the fire, you know how it makes – what was that word again? They gave it to us during violet season.

DOOR. Steam

TUESDAY. Exactly. It's like that, only feelings. Where are you going?

DOOR. We have to tell the king!

TUESDAY. What? No! The king hates magic! The king hates everything!

DOOR. You're telling me that the Lexicographer is going to come here to create *emotional steam*, and I am supposed to lower the bridge for them? Tuesday, don't be foolish. We must warn the king.

TUESDAY. But it might be good magic! Did you think of that?

DOOR. No, silly me. I didn't think of that. Maybe because good magic doesn't exist. That's the whole point of the Lexicographer in the first place! Get rid of "magic." Turn the magic of what happens to water in a warm pot into *steam*. Into *vapor*. This is how they get you, you know. They tease you with a few practical terms like *aglet*, and then before you know it, they chop out your tongue!

TUESDAY. No one is chopping out our tongues.

DOOR. Yet.

(**DOOR** *heads for the door.*)

TUESDAY. Wait, Door, don't! I met someone!

DOOR. Good for you.

Did you lock this from the inside?

TUESDAY. Push.

(*The door opens.*)

Please, wait. I'm – I don't know.

I'm – I met someone at the mead hall. And it's like, I see their hair, right?

And I want to braid it. And then unbraid it.

Really close to my face.

DOOR. They sound like they have great follicles, congratulations.

TUESDAY. They do. The thing is, I can't tell them.

Not until I have the word for it.

It's like asking someone to swim in the grass, otherwise.

I want to hand them the water.

Maybe once I do, something will

happen.

DOOR. Something like what?

TUESDAY. Something like steam.

(**DOOR** *hesitates.*)

Please? I'll protect your tongue, I swear.

DOOR. It's not just about the tongues. It's about –

Remember when you stole that chicken?

TUESDAY. You know I don't like to talk about that –

DOOR. Why not?

TUESDAY. Because I was a bad person.

DOOR. And how does it make you feel?

TUESDAY. Sad. But, sad about existing inside myself. Like a sad that's also a dirty pig and a splintered bridge.

DOOR. Imagine if you had the word for it. And you could say it to yourself over and over and over.

It would be like being trapped in an attic.

TUESDAY. But what about the feeling for when we saw the copper fish?

DOOR. What about it?

TUESDAY. We could have a word for that.

DOOR. Happy.

TUESDAY. Happy but different. Happy but there's mystery and shiny streaks of living things. Imagine the word for that. For how we felt seeing that.

DOOR. What about how it feels to spend all weekend digging outside and muttering under your breath, then going to work Monday morning and realizing that someone wanted to see you, and they had their face pressed to the window, and you didn't even notice. And you can't go back.

TUESDAY. But there's the feeling the next weekend when you split a crusty loaf of bread and dip it in warm garlic.

DOOR. But then there's the feeling the next weekend when you realize that everything from wheat to kin will inevitably perish.

TUESDAY. But then there's the feeling the next weekend when it was supposed to storm and then doesn't.

DOOR. But then there's the feeling the next weekend when you see your neighbor has a garden that far outshines your own.

(Horns sound in the distance.)

TUESDAY. The Lexicographer.

> (**TUESDAY** *makes for the rope to lower the bridge.*)

DOOR. No. Tuesday, no!

> (**DOOR** *fights* **TUESDAY** *for the rope.*)

TUESDAY. Stop it

DOOR. Don't

TUESDAY. We have to let them in.

DOOR. Not if they're going to make us

SAD and ANGRY and WORSE!

We don't know what else there is! We don't know what happens when we give it a name! What if we get tangled in it? It could kill us! And I. Don't. Want. To. Die!

(**TUESDAY** *releases their hold on the rope.*)

TUESDAY. Is that how you feel?

DOOR. We just don't know what could happen. So I feel –

TUESDAY. Afraid.

DOOR. What? What's that? A sort of bug? Is it on me?

TUESDAY. No, it's a word I just made up. For how you're feeling.

DOOR. And how do you know how I'm feeling?

TUESDAY. Because I can hear it in your voice. And it's kind of coming off of you, your skin. And I thought, that's how I'd feel if the Lexicographer left. If they left and I had to wonder if I'd never, ever get the chance to braid anyone's hair. And I thought about prayer, and prayer led to fray, and I thought about a frayed rope, and that led to a frayed anything.

Afraid. It feels kind of right, doesn't it?

DOOR. I guess.

TUESDAY. I think you should say it.

DOOR. Tuesday.

TUESDAY. I think you should say, "I'm afraid."

And I'll make sure nothing happens to your tongue. I'll let you out of the attic.

DOOR. How?

TUESDAY. It's just a word I made up. I'll make up a new one.

Just try it. "I'm afraid."

DOOR. …

I'm afraid.

> (**TUESDAY** *approaches* **DOOR** *slowly and puts their hand on their cheek.* **TUESDAY** *tries to open* **DOOR***'s jaw.)*

DOOR. What are you doing?

TUESDAY. Checking on your tongue.

DOOR. It's fine.

TUESDAY. "I'm afraid."

DOOR. "I'm afraid."

TUESDAY. Does it feel like an attic?

DOOR. It feels like the clearing.

TUESDAY. It's pretty good.

> *(The horns sound. They're very close.* **TUESDAY** *and* **DOOR** *both hold up binoculars. Their jaws drop.)*

TUESDAY & DOOR. Wow

> *(They lower their binoculars.)*

DOOR. It's like seeing the copper fish.

TUESDAY. I wonder what it's called.

DOOR. Let's find out.

> *(**TUESDAY** and **DOOR** look to each other, then to the rope. They take hold. They pull.)*

End of Play

Dugout Daisies

A One Inning Play

by Julissa Mishay Norment

DUGOUT DAISIES was first produced by the 48th Annual Samuel French Off Off Broadway Play Festival at the Vineyard Theater in August 2023. The performance was directed by Cheyenne Parks, and the General Manager was Jaime Jarrett. The cast was as follows:

FEFE..Shalinyah Campbell
TAE ....Sumiaya Nafeesah
Stage Directions......................................Jessica Money

CHARACTERS

FEFE – A fifteen-year-old dark skinned black girl. Genuinely likes playing softball. In uniform with a shirt that says "Dugout Daisies."

TAE – A sixteen-year-old black girl, whose skin is lighter than Fefe's. Couldn't care less about the game or the team. In the same uniform as Fefe.

SETTING

A bench in a dugout.

TIME

Spring. Modern day.

AUTHOR'S NOTES

A Note on Style

(Break) is indicated to take a little time, a breather, make a transition.

Lines that are italicized in brackets [ ] will function as dialogue that serves to not be spoken. Lean into this unspoken dialogue as a mode to live in the subtext of the character.

*(AT RISE: **TAE** and **FEFE** are separated on far sides of a bench. They are in uniform, to whatever degree that means. They are currently in the middle of a girls fast-pitch softball game.)*

TAE. Damn Coach! Just get us out of this inning!

*(**TAE** sits.)*

FEFE. We're supposed to be more than six feet away.

TAE. Are you the bench monitor?

*(**TAE** slides over a good six feet.)*

Like, why does it even matter if we're six feet away? No one at this damn park is even wearing a mask. If there's COVID in the air, I'm pretty sure we all got it.

*(**Break.**)*

God! I'm so over this game.

*(**Break.**)*

Fe, he got you on the bench again?

FEFE. Yeah...

TAE. Wow! Just wow. This coach, he just loves making poor decisions.

FEFE. I know. And I genuinely thought I played last game pretty good.

TAE. You played last game a whole lot better than whoever the hell he got out there now.

FEFE. It just doesn't make sense.

TAE. What doesn't make sense makes dollars.

FEFE. *(Laughing.)* I can't with you. How can you be so chill about everything? It's like you never take anything seriously. I wish I was like that.

TAE. I do be serious.

FEFE. About what? 'Cause it sure ain't about softball.

TAE. I get serious about things that matter to me in the moment. And right now, it's my man and my money.

(Break.)

FEFE. Bro, do you think it's because I struck out last game?

TAE. You still on that?

FEFE. Yes! I worked hard to be out there. But I guess not hard enough.

TAE. *(Matter of fact.)* Maybe. Maybe not. But who cares, regardless if you did good at bat or not, it wouldn't have changed the outcome. We still lost and we're still the worst team in the league.

FEFE. That's for sure. I guess it's hard not to feel like crap because Coach got hella mad.

TAE. When is he *not* hella mad?

FEFE. You right.

TAE. How long have we been in this inning? A girl trying to go home and FaceTime her man.

FEFE. I would say, like…ten minutes?

TAE. We fucking suck…

FEFE. I find it funny how, Coach complains about us losing, but he puts the same people on the field and doesn't bother to change the lineup.

TAE. That part! And he always finds a way to make it our fault. Like Coach…I'm sorry me sitting on the bench is causing *y'all* to lose. But let me not. It's not like I care about this team, anyway, let alone this game. [*And while I'm at it –*]

And it's also annoying being the *only* black girls on this team –

BOTH. And we're both on the bench!

FEFE. *(In a thick southern accent.)* Y'all gotta love Texas girls fast-pitch softball!

TAE. Incorrect.

FEFE. I know for a fact I'm better than Superstar. She always messes up when she's playing second base.

TAE. Oop! There she go again.

BOTH. Error!

TAE. We messy for calling that girl Superstar. I'm sorry but she garbage.

FEFE. Hey, she was the one prancing around here talking about how she's the team's "superstar." Superstar my ass. More like super spoiled.

TAE. What can we say, her dad is the coach.

FEFE. So is yours!

TAE. Okay, first off, he's not my dad. He's my mama's boyfriend, that just so happens to be married to her. And second, he's the *assistant* coach. Big difference.

FEFE. *(Sarcastically.)* Big difference? Pray tell.

TAE. Okay, for starters –

FEFE. Which we not.

TAE. *(Playfully.)* Shut up. Nathaniel he…he's there for… you see what he does is…well damn! He really just there for support.

FEFE. Well hell. By your definition, every parent at this park may very well be the "assistant" coach.

TAE. Nah, if that were the case, I'd like to believe they would at least put us in. You know, to add some spice.

FEFE. Okay! I just think it's bullshit.

TAE. I ain't trippin'.

FEFE. So, you're perfectly okay with him sitting you out every single game?

TAE. How many times I gotta say this? I don't try. Plus, I have an attitude problem, I own that. So what if he doesn't put me in the game.

FEFE. But it's not like you're bad. In practice, you're super fast, you rarely mess up, and…and ugh, you're just naturally athletic!

TAE. I mean, you're not wrong.

FEFE. See! And the fact that you're cool with that, just doesn't sit right with me.

TAE. At the end of the day, I'm living my best life.

FEFE. How? You're one of the best on the team!

TAE. Be that as it may. Like…shit, okay Fe, we don't talk much about it. But it's probably because he doesn't want to show favoritism.

FEFE. Oh, so I guess I'm just guilty by association.

TAE. Now you're projecting. Let's just have fun! Think about it this way, when people see us losing, they don't blame the ones on the bench. If anything, they just feel sorry for us. However, they trash talk the worn-out girls they see playin' all the time! I'm just joining 'em. I look cute, I stay cool and I talk my shit. Period.

FEFE. *(Mumbled.)* Great. More people feeling sorry for me.

TAE. Wait. Who's out here feeling sorry for you?

FEFE. Nothing. It's just…it's just embarrassing. All weekend I haven't gotten any playing time! It's so frustrating being here when my parents come to see.

TAE. If it makes you feel any better, my parents don't care if I play. They just love a good excuse to publicly drink and cut up!

FEFE. *(Giggling.)* Oh no! Not Nathaniel! Not the assistant coach, drinking while coaching.

(They both laugh about this.)

TAE. *(Looking at her shirt.)* And what the *hell* is a dugout daisy?

FEFE. Girl, I don't know.

TAE. Coach really thought he was doing something with this cruddy name.

*(***TAE*** pulls out her phone.* ***FEFE*** *walks towards the fence and observes the game for a moment.)*

FEFE. Ain't no way we're gonna win now…

TAE. Win? We're better off forfeiting.

(Looking up from her phone.) Like girl, when I tell you boys are so freaking stupid. I mean they are *really* so freaking stupid.

(To her phone.) Like *babe*, what's not clicking? Especially when you're clearly disinterested in them, they think it's an act. Like, no… I'm not matching your energy because you're a lame ass nigga.

FEFE. *(Confused.)* Okay?

TAE. It's true, niggas nowadays are so cringy. Yes! We're out of the inning!

FEFE. No, that was our first out.

TAE. I'm sick.

*(**TAE** paces around.)*

Can I just FaceTime my man? That's all I'm asking.

FEFE. Y'all have any special plans this weekend?

TAE. No, he's on lockdown. We haven't seen each other in like, months.

FEFE. Dang, and y'all don't even see each other at school?

TAE. School? Girl nah, he in jail.

FEFE. Then how were you gonna FaceTime him?

TAE. A lot of people don't know this, but inmates be having phones in jail.

FEFE. That's a hoax.

TAE. Girl, I'll FaceTime him right now! Oh shit, I think Coach just saw me with my phone... Damn!

FEFE. Stop cussin' so loud before he makes me do some too!

*(**TAE** puts the phone away, drops and does ten push-ups.)*

What did he do to wind up in jail?

TAE. Don't say it like that. You making it sound like he was at fault...

FEFE. I mean he's in jail for a reason, right?

TAE. In all actuality, they got him by saying he was scamming. But I swear to god that's not true!

FEFE. Okay, pyramid scheme aside, how old is he if he's in jail?

TAE. Twenty.

FEFE. Oh my god.

TAE. Girl I know! Ah! Hey, cover me real quick.

(**FEFE** *grabs an idle bat and starts practice swinging in a slow motion to distract.* **TAE** *pulls back out her phone and attempts to call her man. She lays down on the bench and squeals in delight. At first* **FEFE** *is annoyed with this stunt. But she soon gets into the zone, she is having fun pretending to be at bat again. Lights fade into a single spotlight on* **FEFE** *as the phone chime orchestrates* **FEFE**'s *memory and the journey of her last at bat. The phone chimes build into a cacophony that echoes the pressure, intensity, and rush of a hard battle at bat, and then* **FEFE** *suddenly striking out. The phone rings for its final time ending the at bat.* **FEFE** *stops swinging and sits back on the bench with her head hanging low, while* **TAE** *quickly puts the phone away and sits up in disappointment. Both* **GIRLS** *are back to their usual state: high-strung, on the bench, mindlessly watching the game.)*

They really ain't got no business being out there this long.

FEFE. I have to ask. Isn't it a little weird? With your man and all?

TAE. What's so weird about it?

FEFE. Just the fact that we're fifteen and he's grown.

TAE. He's not that grown. And I'm sixteen, for your information.

FEFE. I'm sorry, no need to be pressed about it.

TAE. I'm not pressed. I'm completely unbothered. And it's totally normal for girls to have older boyfriends.

FEFE. I guess. It just comes off as weird.

TAE. Well, it's not your relationship. So, your comfortability doesn't matter.

FEFE. I'm just looking out for you.

TAE. Thanks boo, but I have parents and an older sister for that.

　(Break.)

He slid into my DMs flexing, giving me attention. You know how it goes…then the next thing I know he practically sent me his whole wallet. To be honest, that's mostly why I started being with him to begin with.

FEFE. Damn, really? It's like that?

TAE. Yes girl. But I'm talking to like four other dudes right now too. So, it doesn't even feel like a relationship.

FEFE. *(Snaps fingers.)* C'mon building a roster.

TAE. A whole lineup! Some of them may be cute, but *never*, I mean never let them know that. My sister gave me three straight rules to live by. One, drain his pockets. Two, keep 'em guessing and three, don't ever catch feelings!

FEFE. *(Amused.)* Never. Does that actually work?

TAE. Hell yeah! I'm talkin' nine times out of ten.

FEFE. Must be nice. I can't even get one guy to talk to me.

TAE. Can I keep it a buck?

FEFE. What?

TAE. *(Rolling her eyes.)* Can I be honest with you?

FEFE. Oh! Of course.

TAE. The reason guys don't talk to you is…they probably think you a lesbian. You kind of give off lesbian vibes.

FEFE. What makes you say that?

TAE. You play softball. *[Duh.]*

FEFE. Screw you! You're on the exact same team as me.

TAE. Yeah, but I'm me and you're you...you know what I mean?

FEFE. No, I don't know what you mean.

TAE. Okay well... *[How should I say this?]*

Maybe it's not that you seem like a lesbian. But you're probably not their preference. Like, look-wise.

(**FEFE** *stares blankly at her.*)

Like for instance, Devin not wanting to go to the dance with you.

FEFE. He said his mom wouldn't let him go.

TAE. That was a lie. We both saw him there...with who?

FEFE. Melody. *[Fuck...]*

TAE. A whole white girl!

FEFE. Damn! All the black guys I know are either gay or with white girls.

TAE. Preference, you see?

FEFE. I don't know! How am I supposed to know what types of vibes I give off? Face it, no one likes me because I'm a weird black girl.

TAE. I'm a weird black girl too. I just know how to hide it better.

FEFE. I don't want to hide it! I just want to be me – you wouldn't understand. Things like this don't apply to you. You're light skinned so everything you do is instantly more attractive.

TAE. That's false. And it's not like I'm yellow boned. I'm just a little bit more lighter than you.

FEFE. Regardless, just a little bit makes a substantial difference!

TAE. I don't agree! My shade range has nothing to do with how *I'm* perceived. If anything, it's all this charisma, uniqueness, nerve and talent! Not even gonna lie to you.

FEFE. Um bitch, racism says hi! Please don't sit up here and act new to black girl struggles!

(Mocking.) "My shade range has nothing to do with how I'm perceived," you sound mad dumb!

TAE. Now you really got me fucked up! You don't know what I go through on a day to day. So don't pretend that you do.

FEFE. Oh? Because your life is so hard as a pretty *light skinned* girl! My bad! Sorry to assume you don't have issues because you have it *so* hard.

TAE. Babe, what is your issue?

FEFE. You want to know what my issue is? It's you Tae! You have it so easy it's exhausting. You don't care about anything because you have the privilege not to care!

TAE. Girl bye. No one trying to hear you player hate on the sidelines because you're bitter. Talking about since I'm "light skinned" I can't possibly understand. Sis, grow up! When it comes to this, who has it worse, light skins or dark skins? Believe it or not, we both have it the same. I wish it weren't true but it is. If we take a look at things carefully though, you ain't even that dark! Or maybe you are, but that's on you sweetheart, not me. But the gag is, it seems that little Fefe just wants to be me.

FEFE. No. The truth is, you will never know what it's like to be in my skin. Why? We are not the same. You don't have to wake up every morning and have to justify your existence. You can just be! How does it feel to be so close to whiteness, but black enough to be everyone's desired choice? Girls like you make me hate what I see in the mirror! I hate you! I hate you because you remind me of how much I hate myself. You're pretty, athletic, funny and chill. You don't know what it's like. You have this imagined idea but you not even close. Like you're supposed to be my friend. Like couldn't you tell I lied to you? Could you not see it on my face that Devin's mom was not the reason he didn't go to the dance with me? He said he didn't want to go with me because I was too dark! You will never know that type of humiliation. And to think, that was just the beginning... Do you know how many games I sat on this bench and thought, I'm too ugly, I don't look like them, I can't possibly fit in. I can't even relate with my own friend... I'm just too dark! And I really thought damn...maybe it's for the best, I'll sit out and stay out of the sun. That comment made me question the thing I love the most. Yeah, I'm probably on the bench because I struck out here or there...but when I leave this dugout it feels like I'm always striking out. No matter how hard I try I'm still not enough. Hmm? Why am I not enough?

TAE. Damn, Fe I had no idea... you know you playing softball has nothing to do with nigga's stupidity, right? I was wrong for suggesting that... I was wrong for suggesting a lot of things.

FEFE. It's just so hard, you know. I hate being here, I hate feeling small. I don't want to feel like this anymore...

> (**FEFE** *lies down on the bench.* **TAE** *sits down beside her and lets* **FEFE** *rest on her lap.* **TAE** *strokes her hair.*)

TAE. It's crazy...for girls like us, there is always this unspoken rule that we have to be excellent all the time. But to be real we don't. And we damn sure don't have to be perfect... I guess I subconsciously built this wall so no one can hurt me. But at the same time I didn't realize I've been hurting you in a way. I don't know how you feel, but I'm here, Fe.

> (*There is a silence on the bench.*)

TAE. Do you really hate me?

FEFE. *(Sitting up.)* No... I was just... I said that out of anger. It's hard not to be envious of you.

TAE. Well, don't okay.

FEFE. Okay.

TAE. Friends?

FEFE. Friends.

> *(The phone rings.)*

You better get that it's your man!

TAE. Chile, let it ring. I think it's almost –

BOTH. Ballgame!

> *(They both laugh and run out of the dugout together.)*

End of Game and End of Play

Freestyle Hand Entry

by Elise Wien

FREESTYLE HAND ENTRY was first produced by Liza Couser and Elise Wien as part of the 48th Annual Samuel French Off Off Broadway Short Play Festival in August 2023. The performance was directed by Liza Couser. The cast was as follows:

CHES . . . . Gabby Policano

CHARACTERS

CHES – A genderqueer teen to young adult.

*The actor who plays Ches must be genderqueer/nonbinary/genderfluid/trans.

SETTING

The JCC locker room.

*(**CHES**, a genderqueer young adult, addresses us.)*

(They might be doing their hair or getting ready for the day.)

(They might be soaking wet, fresh out of the pool or shower.)

(They speak with familiarity and comfort.)

CHES. Seventh grade was a big year for me.

It began when my Nana, who lived across town, started getting leg cramps in the middle of the night. She'd roll over and wake up screaming. It scared my Papa so they moved in with my mom and me. They took my bedroom and I slept on the pull-out couch. Nights, Papa whispered "hey champ" from the doorway and I escorted him to the bathroom for his midnight leak.

The time came when Mom couldn't tend to Nana and Papa and me all at once, so she hauled us to Activity Day at the JCC. We walked down the bannered aisle and at the end was Swim Coach Sydney, sat at her folding table, palms laid flat, tapping and tapping her red acrylic nails, which sprung out like shrimp tails from the end of each finger.

*(**CHES** taps-taps-taps their nails.)*

I would have done anything to spend time with Sydney and her talons.

Including, I guess, join swim team.

Go Stingrays.

Nana and Papa chose a class called Exploring World Cultures Through Dance – movement would be good for Nana's leg, and they wanted to touch again. Her pain had relegated him to the tiniest sliver of bed and Papa needed a way to inch closer.

Every week after that, my mom dropped us off at the JCC, Nana and Papa went to dance, I went to swim practice, then she'd pick us all up and drive home.

Nothing in the world made me hungrier than those swim practices. There was a full body exhaustion that dragged me out of the pool and moved me like a jellyfish – no brain, just a baglike form, pushed down the halls by a current.

In the rec room, rich with the smell of chlorine, I'd eye the vending machines while we waited for pickup.

I begged Nana and Papa for quarters. Papa obliged. I liked to get Bugles because those –

> (**CHES** *rips open a bag of Bugles.**)

You can put them on the ends of your fingers and pretend you have the most delicate hands.

> (**CHES** *places one Bugle at the end of each finger.*)

Anyway, week after week, Nana, Papa, and I would sit in the rec room and they would tell me about their classes:

> (**CHES** *imitates Nana and Papa:*)

Hungarian Folk Dancing

Butoh

Bachata

---

* A license to produce *Freestyle Hand Entry* does not include a license to publicly display any branded logos or trademarked images. Licensees must acquire rights for any logos and/or images or create their own.

And I would tell them about swim:

When you're doing butterfly, you want to raise your chest.

Coach Sydney believes in proper stroke form, so she'll have us get out of the pool and she'll tap the girls' sternums and say, "This wants to be curved upward like sirens on the bows of ships."

God, I wanted her to touch my chest like that.

God, I wanted to be the nail and the chest all at once.

Instead, I asked Papa for quarters and put the Bugles on my fingers, then munched them off one by one.

And then one day, we reached the last bag of Bugles in the machine. And I put in a dollar twenty-five. And the bag didn't budge.

And I crouched down and I reached through the vent to try and wrestle the corn chips out.

And Nana and Papa *freaked out*

They were all:

CHES!!!!

CHES NO!!!!!

CHES YOU'RE GONNA LOSE A HAND!!!!!

And something, a little drop that was already inside me, grew into a puddle, then a creek, an undulating river of desire.

God, I wanted my hand cut off.

Gooooood, I wanted to lose my hand so bad.

The swim team boys shaved their bodies – the *fast* boys shaved their bodies – to reduce drag. I had just begun sprouting hair on my knuckles, and I'd shave them because I didn't have to look at my face that often but I had to see my hands all the time.

I had a friend on the swim team, Jeremy, who was really into transplant videos.

On YouTube, if you watch Dr. Pimple Popper, autoplay will go from pimple popper videos to cyst draining videos and then eventually it'll serve you a full face transplant, where, if the face is fresh enough, they can connect all the nerves and you can get a new face – someone else's face – where your face once was.

On this channel, there's a short documentary about a man with two left hands. He lost his hand in a carpentry accident and the only fresh hands they had were left.

...

...

The documentary said, statistically, men lose their hands more than women.

But if more men lose their hands than women

But there's an equal number of braindead men and women in the hospital

Then some men would have to get women's hands

Just mathematically.

So that's something I thought about a lot.

Actually.

I thought, if I could get my hand mangled by the vending machine in the rec room of the JCC of Mid-Westchester, I might get a woman's hand instead.

So week after week I would shove my hand into the machine and Nana and Papa would yell, Ches NOOOOOOOOO.

I watched the two of them partner on the most intimate exercises in the rec room: Papa's arms shaking to hold

Nana in a dip, Nana's fingers massaging her cramped calf. Every week I was reminded how fragile their bodies are as they creaked through:

Hungarian Folk Dancing

Butoh

Bachata.

I watched Papa's arthritic hands curl around the quarters he gave me.

They were in pain, I could see. How could I be so ungrateful of my swimmer's body, my swimmer's hands, when they worked so well?

And it would be a really long time until I sat in a doctor's office and they asked me about self-harm and I said no no nothing like that.

And it would be longer before I realized, yeah, something like that.

Actually

There was something like that.

So it was a difficult time:

Me, flirting with mutilation, and Nana and Papa, the human bumper lanes to keep me safe from the machine's violent maw, and us all, staring out the window of the rec room of the JCC of Mid-Westchester, waiting to be taken home.

And one evening, while we were in our routine, a slight man passed through the rec room on his way to the chapel.

He was frum, in a yami and peyes, he walked with great posture and his head held high.

And from his long black sleeve came a flash of red and I saw that it was my swim coach. Sydney.

And it took me a few weeks to work up the courage to ask her about what I'd seen. I *idolized* Sydney and I didn't want to upset her.

But after a while I couldn't take not knowing and I asked, was that you?

And she said, when I swim, I'll be a woman.

And when we need a minyan, I'll be a man.

And I said, that's *allowed*????

And she said, yeah I'm fluid.

Fluid.

Of course.

Because we were swimmers.

That week, the true miracle happened. Baruch HaShem, someone rolled a dolly into the rec room, opened up the vending machine, and restocked it all. I sat on the bench with a sense of clarity blooming all around me while Nana and Papa, in the background, swayed and swayed.

All of us floating, and fluid, and on our way home.

End of Play

Nub City, USA!

by Nicholas Hulstine

NUB CITY, USA! premiered at the 48th Annual Samuel French Off-Off Broadway Play Festival at the Vineyard Theatre in New York City in August 2023. The play was directed by Jon McCormick. The cast was as follows:

GLEN . . . . Michael Hauschild
DWAYNE . . . . Adam Couperthwaite

CHARACTERS

GLEN – Thirties, overthinks everything because he's a wee bit slow.
DWAYNE – Thirties, just a tad smarter.

SETTING

Rural America.

TIME

Present.

*(Lights up. Two **MEN** in hunting gear. One of them, **DWAYNE**, points a shotgun at the other, **GLEN**, who has his left arm stretched out. After a tense moment –)*

GLEN. I can't –

DWAYNE. Why not –

GLEN. It ain't as easy as you think it is!

DWAYNE. You gotta different way?

GLEN. Why like this?

DWAYNE. Would you quit bein' such a damn pussy and put your arm up?

*(**DWAYNE** aims his rifle at **GLEN**.)*

GLEN. I ain't even understand how this all is suppose to work anyways.

DWAYNE. God damnit Glen, we've been over this for damn near a month now.

GLEN. Well you ain't done a good 'nuff job 'splainin' it then.

DWAYNE. Open your damn ears this time –

GLEN. They is open!

DWAYNE. You said you need money, this is how we get money –

GLEN. But how, this don't make sense?

DWAYNE. Oh my God!

GLEN. Just tell me again…please?

DWAYNE. We took out a half-million dollar life insurance policy on you.

GLEN. Yeah but... That's for if ya end up dyin', n'it?

(**DWAYNE** *takes a deep breath, calms himself.*)

DWAYNE. I'm afraid I ain't been very clear and I blame myself for this and I apologize.

GLEN. Thank ya Dwayne I appreciate that.

DWAYNE. The policy we took out on you, has what's called a dismemberment clause.

GLEN. What's that?

(**DWAYNE** *is obviously frustrated.*)

DWAYNE. Do you remember the drive out here at all?

GLEN. Sure do, it was actually really pretty.

DWAYNE. The clause states that if there is a significant loss of a major limb that the policy will pay out in full even if there is no death.

GLEN. What's a clause?

DWAYNE. It's a separate, thing, like a rule, like an offshoot of the main rule.

GLEN. So like a smaller rule –

DWAYNE. Exactly, but no less important.

GLEN. What's a minor limb?

DWAYNE. A what?

GLEN. You said loss of a major limb, so what's a minor limb then? Cuz I think all my limbs are major.

DWAYNE. I dunno, maybe they mean like a finger or somethin'.

GLEN. Well them's are called digits, everyone knows that.

DWAYNE. Oh everyone knows that? – Can we just do this already!?

(**GLEN** *prepares himself as* **DWAYNE** *raises the shotgun.*)

GLEN. It's gonna bleed a lot though, ain't it?

DWAYNE. I brought the tourniquet fer such a dilemma.

GLEN. Like how much blood?

DWAYNE. Dunno, I reckon probably a pretty good amount.

GLEN. Oh god!

DWAYNE. Are you afraid of blood now?

GLEN. I ain't never seen a lot of it.

DWAYNE. We've been huntin' hundreds of times –

GLEN. Them's deers and such. This is own my human blood.

(**DWAYNE** *lowers the rifle.*)

DWAYNE. We are ten minutes from the truck and twenty minutes from the hospital. And at the hospital they'll shoot you up with so much fucking morphine you'll feel like you're flyin'. Did you seriously not hear a word in the truck?

GLEN. It was so dang pretty out. Little bit of snow, the hills and all them trees. Dolly's Christmas album was on the radio for fuck sakes!

DWAYNE. Do you get everything now?

GLEN. ...Yeah... I get it.

(**DWAYNE** *raises the shotgun and takes aim at* **GLEN**. **GLEN** *stops him again.*)

DWAYNE. What?!

GLEN. How do you know it's gonna work?

DWAYNE. With this ammo? Figure if I shoot just slightly below the elbow, it should blow the forearm off –

GLEN. I mean – like how do we know the clause will work and all?

(DWAYNE lowers the shotgun and searches for a tactic.)

DWAYNE. Did you see those guys at the gas station? They were all missin' arms or legs? This whole town has people missin' a limb. That's why we came here.

(GLEN still looks confused.)

My wife's cousin told me that this insurance company here will give you a life insurance policy for damn near anything. Hunting trips, boating trips, fucking vacations to Disney World. And one day some dude actually read the policy and found the dismemberment clause and was like "who needs two arms?" And it worked. He got five hundred thousand dollars and like a house down in Mexico Beach.

GLEN. You trust your wife's cousin?

DWAYNE. Hell no, he's a complete idiot, but I did a little digging around and sure enough, people are still doing it. That's why they call this place Nub City.

GLEN. Well why am I the one gettin' a limb blowed off, why can't it be you?

DWAYNE. It was you that said you needed money. At the bar, you told me –

GLEN. I know what I said –

DWAYNE. Then what's to know?

GLEN. Why am I givin' you half then?

DWAYNE. Cuz of the risk factor –

GLEN. Just seems we could blow off your arm and split it down half and it be the same as me doin' it. We got a policy on you too.

DWAYNE. We had to otherwise it coulda looked suspicious.

GLEN. So?

DWAYNE. I gotta be able to drive the forklift at the yard.

GLEN. What you need to drive a forklift for if you got all that money?

DWAYNE. It's not like we just walk into the hospital and they just hand us five hundred thousand dollars.

(Beat. GLEN is deep in thought.)

You didn't actually think we'd just get a shit ton of money once we got to –

GLEN. No, I just... I'm tryin' to make one good decision, for once in my life... I've made so many bad ones.

(Beat. DWAYNE sets the gun down.)

DWAYNE. You was sayin' at the bar that the kids haven't been to the doctors since they was born. You ain't seen one since you was in diapers... You can blame yourself all day for the things you think you should've done. But when did you ever have help? We never had a leg up when it came to anything. My parents barely went to grade school. Didn't help in them making good decisions I s'pose. And they didn't help me, just like your parents. They ain't no pullin' yourself up by your bootstraps, that just somethin' rich people say to poor people. All there is, is the cycle of shit. But now we're in a position to help our kids. They young enough, they might not even remember livin' in a single-wide. They'd have doctors, new clothes, maybe some money when they get older. We can end the cycle of shit right now.

(Beat.)

GLEN. Gonna buy a convenience store with my money. Then buy another once it does good, then have a whole fleet of 'em. Leave one to each kid. Glen's Convenience Store: "Because everyone / needs convenience" –

DWAYNE. / Needs convenience –

GLEN. It's a good slogan –

DWAYNE. It's a great slogan.

*(Beat. **GLEN** stands up.)*

GLEN. You're sure this is gonna work?

*(**DWAYNE** stands up.)*

DWAYNE. Brother, this is America! Only in the U.S. of fuckin' A can you blow off an arm and they give you half a million bucks!!

*(Pause. It's setting into **GLEN**'s head now.)*

GLEN. ...Okay.

DWAYNE. Okay?

GLEN. Fuck yeah I am!

DWAYNE. Yeah!!!

GLEN. I'm ready!

DWAYNE. You ready baby?! You ready?!

GLEN. I'M FUCKING READY!! LET'S FUCKING GOOOOOOOO!

DWAYNE. U-S-A! / U-S-A!

GLEN. U-S-A! U-S-A!

*(**GLEN** puts his left arm out and **DWAYNE** raises the shotgun. **DWAYNE** takes aim and pulls a bullet into the chamber.)*

AMERICAAAAAAAA!!!!!

(Blackout:)

(A gunshot rings out in the darkness.)

The Velociraptor's Very Good Day

by Sarah Kaufman
& Shane Dittmar

THE VELOCIRAPTOR'S VERY GOOD DAY was originally created and presented as part of the Musical Theater Lab program at NYC's Prospect Theater Company (www.ProspectTheater.org).

THE VELOCIRAPTOR'S VERY GOOD DAY was originally produced as part of the SOUND BITES Festival in New York City by Theatre Now New York, www.tnny.org.

Written for the 2022 Prospect Musical Theatre Lab, *THE VELOCIRAPTOR'S VERY GOOD DAY* premiered on November 17th, 2022 at Symphony Space as part of *Caption This: 2022 Prospect Musical Theatre Lab in Concert*.

THE VELOCIRAPTOR'S VERY GOOD DAY was presented on May 8th, 2023 at Kaufman Music Center's Merkin Hall as part of Theatre Now! New York's *Sound Bites X: 10th Annual Festival of 10-Minute Musicals*.

THE VELOCIRAPTOR'S VERY GOOD DAY was subsequently produced at the 48th Annual Samuel French Off Off Broadway Short Play Festival in August 2023. The cast was as follows:

RILEY	Aubrey Clyburn
BROTHER	Cameron Walker
MOM	Emy Ramos

CHARACTERS

RILEY – 11–16; G3–E5; any gender; likes dinosaurs; is Autistic. Also plays **VELOCIRAPTOR**. Must be played by an Autistic actor.

BROTHER – 16–19; D3–A4; male; all the self-centered apathy of a guy his age, but with a good heart. Also plays **TRICERATOPS**.

MOM – 40–60; G3–G5; female; beleaguered but kind. Also plays **TYRANNOSAURUS**.

SETTING

The Kitchen Table.

TIME

The Cretaceous Period.

AUTHOR'S NOTES

We encourage the actor playing Riley to explore what an Autistic physicality is for them, focusing on authenticity as opposed to reproducing a stereotypical or expected performance of Autism.

SPECIAL THANKS

They & Them would like to thank Dev Bondarin, Jennifer Blood, Nissa Kahle, Joshua L.K. Patterson, Louisa Nickel, Emy Ramos, Kevin Scheuring, Cameron Walker, Jessica Wu, and especially Aubrey Clyburn, the first and forever Riley, for their contributions to this piece.

*(Lights up on a beautiful morning in the Cretaceous Period. The **VELOCIRAPTOR**, as played by **RILEY**, stretches big and lets out a yawn.)*

[SONG #1 – "A VERY GOOD DAY"]

VELOCIRAPTOR.
>WHAT A DAY
>TO BE A DINOSAUR!
>THERE'S A WHOLE BIG WORLD
>TO EXPLORE!
>
>THE SUN IS OUT, THE FLOWERS BLOOM,
>AND THERE'S LOTS OF PREY I CAN CONSUME
>WITH MY EIGHTY TEETH AND RAZOR CLAWS.
>SOME TASTY MEAT BETWEEN MY JAWS
>
>WILL HELP THIS YOUNG DINO TO GROW,
>AND SOMEHOW I JUST KNOW
>IT'S GONNA BE A VERY GOOD
>
>DAY DAY DAY 'N DAY DAY
>DAY 'N DAY DAY
>DAY DAY DAY 'N DAY DAY
>DAY 'N DAY DAY
>DAY DAY DAY 'N DAY DAY
>DAY 'N DAY DAY
>DAY, DAY, DAY!

>*(**VELOCIRAPTOR** walks over to visit a still-asleep **TRICERATOPS**, played by **RILEY'S BROTHER**.)*

Oh hey Triceratops! Are you feeling horny today?

TRICERATOPS. *(Groggily.)* Velociraptor, I promise you that doesn't mean what you think it does.

VELOCIRAPTOR. Isn't it a beautiful day?

TRICERATOPS. A beautiful day to stay in my cave and sleep, maybe.

VELOCIRAPTOR. Come on! The sand is warm between our dinosaur toes, there isn't a cloud in the Cretacious sky, and I have a good feeling about today!

TRICERATOPS. Ugh, you're talking so loud!

VELOCIRAPTOR. Wanna come with me to visit Tyrannosaurus Rex, the biggest and coolest apex predator we know?

TRICERATOPS. Only if we don't have to sing about it.

VELOCIRAPTOR. *(Devastated.)* But...

TRICERATOPS. Okay, fine, but make it quick.

VELOCIRAPTOR. Okay!!!

TRICERATOPS. *(Under his breath.)* Jesus.

VELOCIRAPTOR.
WHAT A DAY
TO BE A DINOSAUR!

TRICERATOPS.
YOUR VOLUME MAKES
THIS DINO SORE.

VELOCIRAPTOR.
BUT WE'RE OFF TO SEE OUR BESTEST FRIEND.

VELOCIRAPTOR & TRICERATOPS.
WE'LL BE BUDDIES TO THE END,
SO IT'S GONNA BE A VERY GOOD

VELOCIRAPTOR.	**TRICERATOPS.**
DAY DAY DAY 'N DAY DAY	DAY DAY DAY DAY
DAY 'N DAY DAY	DAY DAY DAY DAY

DAY DAY DAY 'N DAY DAY	DAY DAY DAY DAY
DAY 'N DAY DAY	DAY,
DAY DAY DAY 'N DAY DAY	DAY DAY DAY DAY
DAY 'N DAY DAY	DAY DAY DAY DAY
DAY, DAY, DAY!	DAY, DAY, DAY!

> *(They travel across the landscape towards the cave belonging to **TYRANNOSAURUS**, played by **RILEY'S MOM**.)*

VELOCIRAPTOR. *(Calling into the cave.)* Tyrannosaurus!

TYRANNOSAURUS. *(Emerging cheerily from within.)* Hi Velociraptor, Triceratops!

TRICERATOPS. Tyrannosaurus, can you tell Velociraptor to keep it down this early in the morning?

TYRANNOSAURUS. Oh Triceratops, you know Doctor Caplan says Velociraptor has a little trouble communicating, so we have to be extra patient and kind. After all…

>DINOSAUR FRIENDS ARE FOREVER,
>STORMY SKIES OR PICTURE-PERFECT WEATHER.
>WE'LL HELP EACH OTHER OUT THROUGH WHATEVER,
>THE THREE OF US WILL STICK TOGETHER!

ALL.
>DINOSAUR FRIENDS ARE FOREVER,
>STORMY SKIES OR PICTURE-PERFECT WEATHER.
>WE'LL HELP EACH OTHER OUT THROUGH WHATEVER,

VELOCIRAPTOR & TYRANNOSAURUS.	**TRICERATOPS.**
THE THREE OF US WILL STICK TOGETHER!	THE THREE OF US…

> *(**TRICERATOPS** breaks off his last word…)*

TRICERATOPS.
>HEY, WHAT'S THAT BIG THING IN THE SKY?

TYRANNOSAURUS.
IT'S NOTHING THAT WE CAN'T GET BY!
'CAUSE AS LONG AS WE STAY ONE,

TYRANNOSAURUS & TRICERATOPS.
TWO,

ALL.
THREE,
I CAN ALMOST GUARANTEE
IT'S GONNA BE A VERY GOOD

(The three **FRIENDS** *celebrate and clap along to their layered chorus.)*

VELOCIRAPTOR.	**TRICERATOPS.**	**TYRANNOSAURUS.**
DAY DAY DAY 'N DAY DAY	DAY DAY DAY DAY	DAY DAY
DAY 'N DAY DAY	DAY DAY DAY DAY	DAY DAY
DAY DAY DAY 'N DAY DAY	DAY DAY DAY DAY	DAY DAY
DAY 'N DAY DAY	DAY,	DAY,
DAY DAY DAY 'N DAY DAY	DAY DAY DAY DAY	DAY DAY
DAY 'N DAY DAY	DAY DAY DAY DAY	DAY DAY
DAY, DAY, DAY!	DAY, DAY, DAY!	DAY, DAY, DAY!

(They get into it, starting to riff and ad-lib. It really is going to be a very good...)

DAY DAY DAY 'N DAY DAY	DAY DAY DAY DAY	DAY DAY
DAY 'N DAY DAY	DAY DAY DAY DAY	DAY DAY
DAY DAY DAY 'N DAY DAY	DAY DAY DAY DAY	DAY DAY
DAY 'N DAY DAY	DAY,	DAY,

DAY DAY DAY 'N DAY DAY	DAY DAY DAY DAY	DAY DAY
DAY 'N DAY DAY	DAY DAY DAY DAY	DAY DAY
DAY, DAY...	DAY, DAY...	DAY, DAY...

(Instead of a final, triumphant chord, the lights black out as a cacophony of notes sound from the piano. We sit in the dark for a moment before...)

*(The lights come back up on **VELOCIRAPTOR**, stunned, standing between the corpses of **TRICERATOPS** and **TYRANNOSAURUS**, both of whom have been extincted by the asteroid. **VELOCIRAPTOR** scans the stage, noticing the destruction all around, and calls out urgently.)*

VELOCIRAPTOR. Triceratops? Tyrannosaurus? Anybody?

(No response.)

[SONG #2 – "MY FRIENDS ARE DEAD"]

MY FRIENDS ARE DEAD.
THEY WON'T COME TO.
SOME BRIGHT THING IN THE SKY MADE EV'RYBODY DIE.
NOW WHAT AM I SUPPOSED TO DO?

MY FRIENDS ARE COOKED.
LIKE, FULL SAUTÉ.
THEY'RE SEARED DOWN TO THE BONE,
AND NOW THAT I'M ALONE,
WHAT AM I SUPPOSED TO SAY?

NO ONE TO TELL ME TO BE QUIET.
NO ONE TO HUG ME WHEN I'M SCARED.
NO ONE TO HUNT WITH ME,
NO ONE TO BE UPFRONT WITH ME.
WHY AM I THE DINO WHO WAS SPARED?

VELOCIRAPTOR. *(Softly crying in rhythm.)*
> MY FRIENDS ARE GONE. (SNIFF)
> NOW THEY'RE JUST MEAT. (SNIFF, SNIFF)
> AND MY STOMACH STARTS TO GROAN,
> 'CAUSE MY SCHEDULE'S REALLY THROWN.
> BUT WHAT AM I SUPPOSED TO...

Wait!

> *(**VELOCIRAPTOR** looks at their deceased friends quizzically, getting an idea.)*

[SONG #3 – "I MUST BE ME"]

> I'VE BEEN SO BROKEN AND TORN APART,
> I FORGOT WHO I AM IN MY DINOSAUR HEART.
> VELOCIRAPTOR MEANS "SPEEDY THIEF,"
> AND I CAN'T LOSE MYSELF TO THIS HORRIBLE GRIEF.
>
> COME WHAT MAY, I MUST BE ME,
> NO MATTER WHAT DEATH THE SKY SENDS.
> I HAVE THIS GREAT OPPORTUNITY:
> I CAN EAT MY FRIENDS!

> *(**TRICERATOPS** stands back up.)*

TRICERATOPS. Velociraptor!

VELOCIRAPTOR. Triceratops? Is that you?

TRICERATOPS. It's my ghost! You have to eat me, Velociraptor! You have to feast on my flesh!

> *(**TYRANNOSAURUS** stands back up as well.)*

TYRANNOSAURUS. That's right, Velociraptor, you can't let our delicious dinosaur meat go to waste. You have to eat us!

TRICERATOPS.
> YOUR DINOSAUR BUDDIES MAY BE GONE FOR GOOD,
> BUT YOU HAVE TO DO WHAT ANY SCAVENGER SHOULD.

TYRANNOSAURUS.
VELOCIRAPTOR, BE BRAVE AND BOLD,
AND CHEW ON OUR BONES

TYRANNOSAURUS & TRICERATOPS.
BEFORE OUR BODIES GET COLD.

TRICERATOPS & TYRANNOSAURUS.
OOH.

VELOCIRAPTOR.
COME WHAT MAY, I MUST BE ME,

TYRANNOSAURUS.
Eat my tail!

TRICERATOPS & TYRANNOSAURUS.
OOH.

TRICERATOPS.
WE'RE EXTINCT!
BUT

BEFORE THAT BIG ASH CLOUD DESCENDS.

TRICERATOPS & TYRANNOSAURUS.
YOU HAVE THIS GREAT OPPORTUNITY:

Are you sure?

We consent to this!

YOU CAN EAT YOUR FRIENDS!

I CAN EAT MY FRIENDS!

*(As the **THREE** sing, exactly what you think happens begins to happen.)*

ALL.
DINO NUGGETS ARE FOREVER!
STORMY SKIES, OR PICTURE-PERFECT WEATHER.
EAT YOUR FRIENDS, IT'S TOTALLY WHATEVER,
THEN WE'LL ALWAYS BE TOGETHER!
DINO NUGGETS ARE FOREVER!
DINO NUGGETS ARE FOREVER!
DINO NUGGETS ARE FOREVER!

*(The piano cuts out under **VELOCIRAPTOR/
RILEY**'s big note, which they continue to hold
triumphantly. Lights change and we're now
in the family's kitchen, where **RILEY** and
BROTHER sit across from one another at a
table and **MOM** stands by the freezer.)*

*(**RILEY** finishes the song and sits back
proudly. Communication accomplished.)*

MOM. Oh my God, Riley! What in the...

(She takes a deep breath, re-centering.)

Riley, sweetheart, that was a very vivid stor– Do you remember what Doctor Caplan said about how, sometimes, we have to think about what we're saying? Because it can make people feel uncomfortable to think that you want to eat them–

BROTHER. *(Bored.)* Mom. Riley wants Dino Nuggets.

RILEY. Yeah.

MOM. You got that from the cannibalism?

BROTHER. Doctor Caplan's a moron, I don't think Riley has any trouble communicating, people just don't listen.

RILEY. Yeah.

BROTHER. *(To **RILEY**.)* Dinosaur Donner Party? Autism is fucking cool.[*]

RILEY. Yeah.

MOM. *(A little shaken.)* Okay... Dino nuggets it is.

(She opens the freezer and pulls out a bag.)

RILEY. *(Victorious.)* Yes.

---

[*] You may replace the profanity in this line with a minced oath, if that is more appropriate for your production.

BROTHER. Hey, you know what that means?

[SONG #4 – "A VERY GOOD DAY"] – Reprise

IT'S GONNA BE A VERY GOOD

RILEY.	BROTHER.	MOM.
DAY DAY DAY 'N DAY DAY	DAY DAY DAY DAY	DAY DAY
DAY 'N DAY DAY	DAY DAY DAY DAY	DAY DAY
DAY DAY DAY 'N DAY DAY	DAY DAY DAY DAY	DAY DAY
DAY DAY 'N DAY	DAY,	DAY,
DAY DAY DAY 'N DAY DAY	DAY DAY DAY DAY	DAY DAY
DAY 'N DAY DAY	DAY DAY DAY DAY	DAY DAY

ALL.
DINO NUGGETS ARE FOREVER!
DINO NUGGETS!

(Blackout.)

www.ingramcontent.com/pod-product-compliance
Lightning Source LLC
Chambersburg PA
CBHW072017290426
44109CB00018B/2267